Deutfchland ~ Lutherland

STÄTTEN UND GESCHEHNISSE DER DEUTSCHEN REFORMATION

1483 — 1546

OST ~ SEE

NORD ~ SEE

WITTENBERG

KURSACHSEN

Ph. MELANCHTHON

Joh. BUGENHAGEN

D. Martin LUTHER

Casp. CRUCIGER

Nic. AMSDORF

Justus JONAS

For Christine, Nicole, Anna, Rachel, and Mark

Published by Concordia Publishing House

3558 S. Jefferson Avenue

St. Louis, MO 63118-3968

Text copyright © 2004 Paul L. Maier

Illustrations copyright © 2004 Concordia Publishing House

Map on endsheets courtesy of the Stiftung Luthergedenkstätten in Sachsen-Anhalt.

Manufactured in the United States of America

2   3   4   5   6   7   8   9   10   11   13   12   11   10   09   08   07   06   05   04

Martin Luther

A Man Who Changed the World

WRITTEN BY

PAUL L. MAIER

ILLUSTRATED BY

GREG COPELAND

CONCORDIA PUBLISHING HOUSE • SAINT LOUIS

Our loving God helps His people turn from sin and error. In the Old Testament, He sent prophets to warn them. In the New Testament, He even sent His own Son, Jesus Christ, to reform and save the world. And in the centuries since then, God sent others to keep the church pure.

The greatest of these was Martin Luther, an extraordinary man who started the Reformation just when the church needed it most.

Martin was born at Eisleben in Germany in 1483—nine years before Columbus sailed to America! In those days, the Christian church no longer based its beliefs on the Bible alone. It had actually invented new doctrines and practices that Jesus and His apostles had never taught. Sadly, too, the church leaders of that time, far from setting a good example for their people, sinned worse than the people did!

Martin Luther would change all that.

Hans Luther, Martin's father, was a rather prosperous miner, and his mother, Margaretta, was strict when it came to discipline. The family soon moved to Mansfeld, where Martin went to school and learned his lessons in Latin. When he was 14, Martin was sent to school in Magdeburg. There, students who did poorly in their studies were made to wear a donkey mask! After only a year, Hans sent Martin to school in Eisenach. Martin and other students there would go door to door and sing for their food, a custom of young scholars at the time that did not mean they were poor as beggars.

Because his son was so brilliant, Hans enrolled Martin at the University of Erfurt to study law. Martin might have become an important lawyer, but a sudden thunderstorm came along and changed his plans—and church history too! He was returning to the university after visiting his parents when a lightning bolt knocked him to the ground. "Save me, St. Anne!" he cried out. "I will become a monk!"

And he did. Thinking this was a sign from God, Luther sold his law books and entered the Augustinian monastery at Erfurt. Papa Luther was furious: he had hoped his son would be a wealthy lawyer and support him in his old age. Now what would he do?

Martin did not wish to displease his father. He only wanted to lead a holy life and know that his sins were forgiven so he would go to heaven. Brother Martin tried to be a good monk: he prayed long hours, ate little, worked hard, studied constantly, and endured great hardships.

Did all that help? It did not. Luther was surprised and saddened that the harder he tried to keep God's commandments perfectly, the more he felt like a failure.

Perhaps a visit to Rome, the headquarters of the Roman Catholic Church, would help. The monastery sent Brother Luther over the Alps to Italy. But when he saw how worldly and sinfully the pope and the cardinals behaved, his despair only deepened.

Then, once again, Luther's life changed. The ruler of Saxony, Frederick the Wise, had established a new university in Wittenberg, a hundred miles away from Erfurt. Luther was sent there to be a professor.

In Wittenberg Luther became a scholar, professor, and preacher. But had he found peace with God?

The head of the local monastery, Johann von Staupitz, led Luther to the Bible for answers: In St. Paul's letter to the Romans, Luther read that God's righteousness (His holiness) is a *gift* to those who believe in Christ as their Savior. Paul explained that this righteousness was not only God's own perfection, but something that He *gave* to people who were sorry for their sins and believed in Christ. Now Luther understood: he didn't have to earn God's forgiveness because Christ had earned it for him.

Luther was excited to learn this truth and wanted to tell others, but, strangely enough, the church stood in his way.

The church of his time taught that the punishments for sin in a place called purgatory (between heaven and hell) could be removed if people bought what were called *indulgences.* Martin studied the Bible but he could not find these words or concepts—purgatory or indulgences—in its pages. These teachings were not God's teachings. And so, when a man named Tetzel tried to sell such indulgences near Wittenberg, it was too much for Luther.

On October 31, 1517, he wrote 95 concerns (or theses) about purgatory, indulgences, and other teachings of the church—topics on which he would debate anyone. Then he nailed them to the door of the Castle Church in Wittenberg.

It was an act that began the Reformation and changed the world.

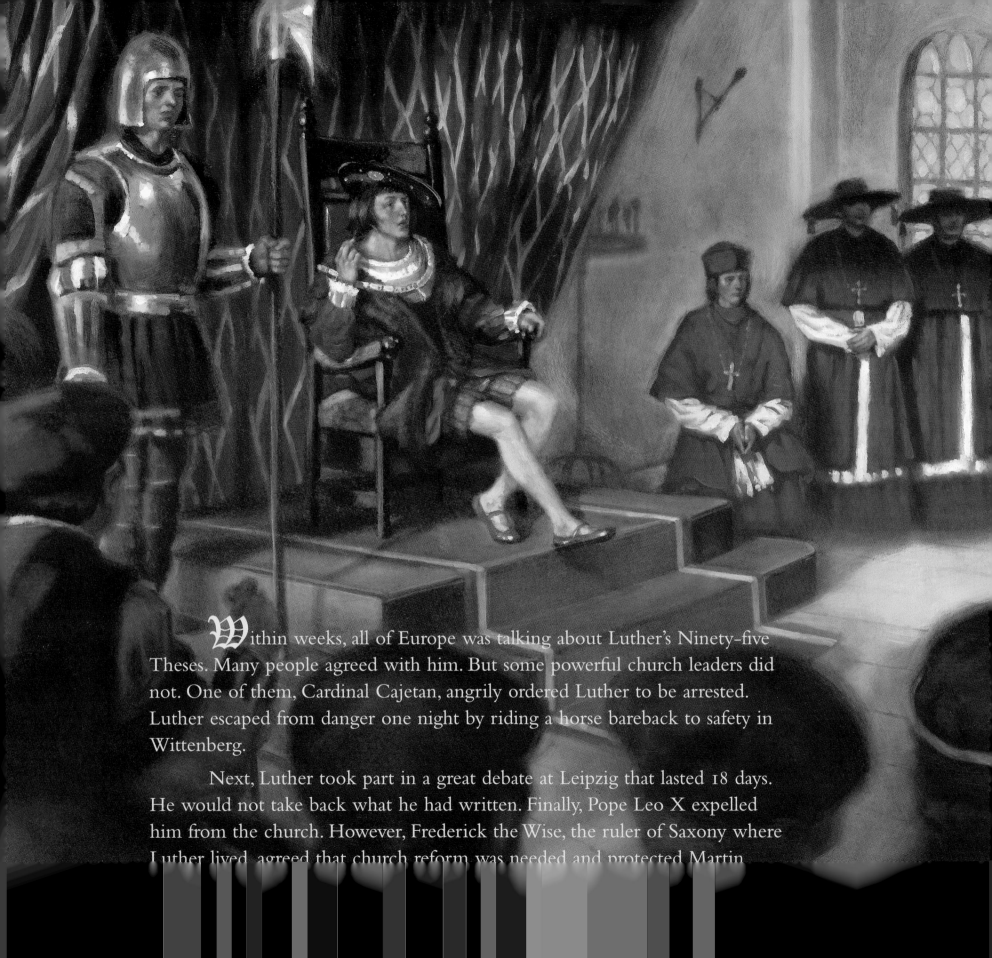

Within weeks, all of Europe was talking about Luther's Ninety-five Theses. Many people agreed with him. But some powerful church leaders did not. One of them, Cardinal Cajetan, angrily ordered Luther to be arrested. Luther escaped from danger one night by riding a horse bareback to safety in Wittenberg.

Next, Luther took part in a great debate at Leipzig that lasted 18 days. He would not take back what he had written. Finally, Pope Leo X expelled him from the church. However, Frederick the Wise, the ruler of Saxony where Luther lived, agreed that church reform was needed and protected Martin

Eventually Luther appeared before Charles V, the emperor over much of Europe, at a city on the Rhine River called Worms. Here, the emperor, his court, and the church leaders demanded that Luther take back what he had written. But Martin replied bravely: "My conscience is captive to the Word of God. I cannot recant anything, for to go against conscience is neither right nor safe. Here I stand. I cannot do otherwise. God help me. Amen!"

Soon afterward, Charles V and the church leaders declared that Luther was an outlaw, and anyone could kill him on sight.

Luther's life was in danger as he traveled home to Wittenberg. Along the way, he and his companions were overtaken by a band of horsemen. Luther was kidnapped! He was taken to the Wartburg, a fortress that loomed over the town of Eisenach.

But the kidnappers were not what they seemed. They were his friends in disguise. Frederick had planned the "kidnapping" to hide Martin from his enemies.

The months Luther spent in hiding were lonely, but he was sure God was with him and that he was right to tell others about salvation in Christ.

Luther used his time at the Wartburg wisely. He believed that the best way to teach the Gospel was to let people read it for themselves. (At that time the Bible was in Latin, a language most people could not read.) So he translated the New Testament into the language of the people—German.

Martin stayed in touch with events at home through letters and visits from friends. And when the citizens of Wittenberg begged him to return, he risked his life and bravely left the Wartburg.

Luther's enemies had warned that reforming the church would lead to disorder and chaos. For a while this seemed to be true.

In Wittenberg, a few of the clergy were making too many changes too quickly. Monasteries and nunneries closed. Some people vandalized religious art, music, stained glass, and statues of the saints. Others claimed they had personal "revelations" from God apart from Scripture. Philip Melanchthon, a scholar who was Luther's right-hand man in Wittenberg, cried, "The dam has broken, and I cannot stop the waters."

But Luther could. From the pulpit, he preached against such actions. He explained that teachings and traditions of the church that were against Scripture should be changed. But other practices that helped people in worship—like liturgy and music—should be kept.

Preaching and celebrating the Sacraments were how Luther proclaimed the forgiveness of sins and brought God's Word to the people. And because new inventions made printing faster and cheaper, Luther took full advantage of the press by writing letters, essays, and books. His writings—such as the catechisms and hymns—helped pastors, teachers, parents, and children as they learned and worshiped.

$\mathfrak{N}$ow began some wonderfully happy years in the life of Martin Luther. With false teachings and wrong practices corrected, Luther and his associates prepared many new materials for the church. They published a complete German Bible, new orders of worship, new hymns, prayers, and sermon books. Luther wrote both the *Small* and *Large Catechisms* for teaching children and adults. And since he loved music, he composed some very famous hymns, including the Christmas carol, "From Heaven Above to Earth I Come," and the great hymn of the Reformation, "A Mighty Fortress Is Our God."

Considering all of this, it is no wonder that Luther said he was too busy and set in his ways to become a husband. But that was before he met Katherine von Bora, a former nun.

In agreement with the changes brought on by the Reformation, Katherine had decided to leave her convent. Running away was very dangerous—getting caught would result in beatings and severe punishment. So under the cover of the midnight sky, Katherine and several other nuns climbed into empty fish barrels and hid. The barrels were taken by wagon to Wittenberg where the former nuns started new lives.

Martin and Katie, as he called her, were married in 1525. She was a strong and intelligent woman and was as outspoken as her husband. The Luthers lived a happy life in Wittenberg. Six children—three boys and three girls—added to their joy.

The Reformation was not just one movement in one country that led to one Protestant church body. In England, it led to the Anglican Church. In Switzerland, France, Holland, and Scotland, it became the Reformed Church. Even in Germany, Anabaptists split from Lutherans.

Meanwhile, Emperor Charles V threatened the German Lutheran princes "with fire and sword" if they did not return to the Catholic Church. The Lutheran princes boldly refused and gave Charles a document that began, "We protest. ..." The term "Protestant" was born that day.

Still trying to reconcile, the emperor and the Lutheran leaders met again at Augsburg in 1530. Luther was still considered a criminal and would have been captured and executed had he gone there. Instead, fellow reformer Philip Melanchthon presented a formal statement of what the reformers believed. This statement came to be known as the Augsburg Confession, and it remains the formal expression of Lutheran teachings to this day.

After Augsburg, Luther was busier than ever. Students from all over Europe studied at Wittenberg, then carried his teachings back to their native lands. This is how not only much of Germany, but whole nations also converted, such as Denmark, Norway, Sweden, Finland, and Iceland. Later, when people from these countries moved to America, Australia, and elsewhere, they carried their Lutheran faith with them.

So many students and visitors stayed with the Luthers at Wittenberg that Katie sometimes had trouble finding food and beds for all of them. At mealtimes, Luther amused everyone with his blazing sense of humor. He also made dinnertime observations that were so valuable students wrote down nearly everything he said. These notes were later published in a book called *Luther's Table Talk*.

Luther wrote an astonishing number of letters, articles, pamphlets, studies, and commentaries on books of the Bible. His assembled works have been published in almost *one hundred* fat volumes. Even his enemies admitted that he was a genius.

Luther also had difficulties to face. His health was not always good and his life was in danger should he ever leave Germany. He was angry with German peasants for staging a revolution, reformers who interpreted the Bible incorrectly, and Jews who did not convert to Christianity once the Gospel had been restored. But through it all, Luther knew the peace of God. He knew that as a baptized child of God in Christ.

Early in 1546, Luther went to Eisleben to help solve a quarrel between two princes. He settled the dispute, but the elderly Luther was tired. Before he could start on his journey back to Wittenberg he suffered several heart attacks.

Friends gathered around his bed. One asked, "Reverend Father, are you willing to die in the name of the Christ and the doctrine you have preached?" Luther clearly answered, "Yes!" then passed away. His life had come full circle—he died in Eisleben, where he was born.

Martin Luther was buried beneath the pulpit in the Castle Church at Wittenberg. On the doors of that very church, nearly 30 years before, he had posted the Ninety-five Theses that started the Reformation.

Why are some men and women called "great"? Because their amazing lives have helped make the world better. In that sense, Martin Luther was one of the greatest men who ever lived. His reformation set people free to obey God rather than men and led to the rise of the national state. His Bible translation helped form the modern German language spoken today. His hymns returned singing to the people in the congregation and inspired composers and artists to create their masterpieces. He invented the parsonage, dignified labor as a "calling" from God, and stimulated learning. His writings have influenced the entire world.

But his greatest gift of all was to find in God's Word the answer to the question that had tormented him as a monk: "What must I do to win God's forgiveness for my sins?" The Bible showed him that God had already done it all for him by sending Christ, whose suffering and death paid the penalty for sin and whose resurrection would be shared by all who had faith in Him. That great good news is the Gospel—the central message of the church that is as great today as it was 500 years ago at Luther's time, or in Jesus' own day.

Martin Luther did, indeed, change the world.

OST ~ SEE

NORD ~ SEE

WITTENBERG   KURSACHSEN

Ph. MELANCHTHON   Joh. BUGENHAGEN

D. Martin LUTHER

Casp. CRUCIGER   Nic. AMSDORF   Justus JONAS

Deutschland ~ Lutherland

STÄTTEN UND GESCHEHNISSE DER DEUTSCHEN REFORMATION

1483 — 1546